Be an eco hero

On the move

Sue Barraclough

SEA-TO-SEA
Mankato Collingwood London

This edition first published in 2013 by Sea-to-Sea Publications
Distributed by Black Rabbit Books
P.O. Box 3263, Mankato, Minnesota 56002

Printed in the United States of America, North Mankato, MN

9 8 7 6 5 4 3 2

Published by arrangement with the Watts Publishing Group Ltd, London.

Library of Congress Cataloging-in-Publication Data

Barraclough, Sue.
 Be an eco hero on the move / Sue Barraclough.
   p. cm. -- (Be an eco hero)
 Includes index.
 ISBN 978-1-59771-380-1 (library binding)
 1. Transportation--Environmental aspects--Juvenile literature. 2. Environmentalism--Juvenile literature. I. Title.
 HE147.65.B366 2013
 388.028'6--dc23
                    2011049896

Series editor: Sarah Peutrill
Art director: Jonathan Hair
Design: Big Blu Design
Illustrator: Gary Swift

Credits: Ravind Balavaman/Shutterstock: 27tr. Sarah Bossert/Shutterstock: 15tl. Jacek Chabraszewski/istockphoto: 15b. Chris Fairclough/Franklin Watts: 22, 27b. Jim Fromer/istockphoto: 9tl. Jeff Greenburg/Alamy: 21t. Kim Gunkel/istockphoto: 25bl. Jupiter/Goodshot/Alamy: 10. Kathy Kaplan/istockphoto: 11t. Michael Klinec/Alamy: 23. Krzysztof Kwiafkowski / istockphoto: 18. Gary D. Landesman/Corbis: 16. Leontura/istockphoto: 20. Jeff Ludes/Alamy: 11b. Monkey Business Images/Shutterstock: front cover, 19. David Parsons/istockphoto: 12. David Pearson/Alamy: 25br. Denis Radovanovic/istockphoto: 15tr. Rada Razvan/Shutterstock: 14. Alistair Scott/istockphoto: 9tr. Stephen Strathdee/istockphoto: 7. Tony Tremblay/istockphoto: 6. 21 Archive/istockphoto: 27tl. Vibrant Image Studio/Shutterstock: 21b. Peter Vopenka/Shutterstock: 13. H Mark Weldman/Alamy: 17. Karen Winton/Shutterstock: 11c. Linda Yolanda/istockphoto: 25t. Yvan / Shutterstock: 8.

RD/6000006415/001
May 2012

Contents

Find out ways to help your planet in this book and become an eco hero like me!

Words in **bold** are in the glossary on page 28.

On the Move

Every day, all over the world, we move around in different ways. We walk or ride a bike, but we also travel in vehicles such as cars, buses, trains, and planes.

We also use transport trucks, pickups, and planes to carry things that we need, such as clothing, toys, and food from place to place. Every vehicle needs **fuel** to make it move.

How do you travel around?

Fossil Fuels

Most vehicles run on **gasoline** or **diesel**. These are made from a **fossil fuel** called **oil**. Fossil fuels are made from plant and animal materials. Fossil fuels take millions and millions of years to form under the ground.

An **oil rig** is used to drill down deep below the sea to find oil.

We are using up fossil fuels very quickly. Once we run out of fossil fuels it will take millions of years for more to form.

Fuel is very important to us. Eco heroes don't waste it!

Using Less Fuel

There are many simple things you and your family can do to save fuel.

Be an eco hero by:

• Helping to empty the trunk. If the trunk is full the car is much heavier. The car has to use more fuel if the car is heavy.

• Opening the window instead of asking to use the air conditioning. Air conditioning uses fuel.

• Reminding adults to check tire pressures. Having tires at the right pressure saves fuel.

• Helping to take off roof racks and roof boxes when you do not need them. A roof rack or roof box slows the car down and uses more fuel.

Roof rack

Air Pollution

Most vehicles on the road cause **pollution.** As their engines use fuel, they make **gases** that can poison the air and cause **global warming.**

Ships, airplanes, and some trains also pump out gases that are very bad for the planet.

We breathe in these gases and it can be bad for us. Pollution in the air also mixes with rain. This makes **acid rain**, which can damage trees and buildings.

These trees have been killed by acid rain.

Short Trips

Be an eco hero by cutting down car use. For a short trip, such as going to school, try not to travel by car. See if you can find another way to travel and you will:

• save fuel
• cut down pollution
• help to clean the air.

Walk

Scoot

Skateboard

Run

15

Car Share

Many people use their cars to travel to work and to school. If you make trips like this every day, you could figure out a car sharing **rota.**

Be an eco hero by giving someone a ride or getting one yourself.

If you share a car trip, the car is full rather than carrying just one or two people. This means fewer cars on the road, which causes less pollution. The roads are safer, too.

Riding a Bike

You can be an eco hero by riding a bike.
This is good for the planet and it is also
good for you.

Riding a bike does not use gasoline, does not cause pollution, and keeps you physically fit!

Remember to cycle safely and wear a helmet.

Travel by Bus

You are an eco hero if you travel by bus or **streetcar.** This is a good way to use less fuel and cut down pollution. Traveling by bus or streetcar means less traffic on the roads. A 30-seater bus can mean 30 fewer cars on the road.

If you go on a day trip, try to find out if you can travel by bus. Traveling on a bus with your friends is fun.

Travel by Train

Trains are a fast way to travel around. Train travel can help save fuel, reduce traffic, and cut down pollution. It can also be more fun to travel by train.

Traveling on a train full of people is better than each person traveling in their own car. It cuts down on traffic jams, too.

Eco Shopping

Every day, trucks, planes, and trains **transport** food all over the planet. This makes more traffic, uses fuel, and causes pollution.

Be an eco hero by:

- Reading food labels to find out how far your food has traveled and choosing **local** food if you can. The food will be fresher and you will be helping local farmers.
- Helping to do the grocery shopping online, if this is available in your area.
- Getting toys and clothes delivered to your home.

Choose local food

Shop online

Home delivery

A truck delivering to 50 homes means 50 fewer cars on the road.

ECO Hero Activities

Here are some eco hero activities you could do at home.

Be an eco hero!
Don't travel by car.

Walk, skate, scoot, or cycle instead!

Help your friends be eco heroes! Make a poster to show all the ways to get around without causing pollution. You could use pictures from magazines or the Internet.

Ask an adult to help you write a letter to your local authority asking for more cycle paths and bicycle lanes where you live.

Bicycle lanes make cycling safer.

Learn how your bike works and how to clean and repair it.

Clean bikes last longer.

Glossary

acid rain   Rain that is full of dangerous chemicals.

diesel   A type of fuel.

fossil fuel   Materials found deep under the ground and formed over millions of years from dead animals and plants.

fuel   Material used to make heat or light, usually by being burned. Coal, gas, and oil are types of fuel.

gas   Airlike substance that you cannot see.

gasoline   A type of fuel made from oil.

global warming   Worldwide rise in temperatures affecting sea levels and weather.

local   A person, place, or store that is in your neighborhood.

oil   Thick, dark liquid found deep under the ground.

oil rig   A structure used for drilling for oil.

pollution   Gas or liquid that dirties or poisons air, earth, or water.

rota   A list of dates and times and whose turn it is to do what.

streetcar   A vehicle that runs along a fixed track.

transport   To move people or things from place to place.

Learn More

This book shows you some of the ways you can be an eco hero. But there is plenty more you can do to save the planet. Here are some web sites that have lots of ideas and information to help you learn more about being an eco hero:

www.eia.gov/kids/energy.cfm?page=us_energy_transportation-basics
The U.S. Energy Administration's web site tells you all about using and saving energy for transportation. Then click on Games & Activities to have some educational fun.

http://globalwarmingkids.net/
Find out all about global warming and the things we can all do to tackle it.

http://tiki.oneworld.net/
Find out about climate change with Tiki the penguin.

http://www.kidsforsavingearth.org/
Learn about how kids are saving the Earth and how you can, too, on this colorful web site. You can also order books, eco-friendly cards and gift wrap, posters, and stickers.

Note to parents and teachers: Every effort has been made by the Publishers to ensure that these web sites are suitable for children, that they are of the highest educational value, and that they contain no inappropriate or offensive material. However, because of the nature of the Internet, it is impossible to guarantee that the contents of these sites will not be altered. We strongly advise that Internet access is supervised by a responsible adult.

Index